*The Curious Little Critters™ Series

Ask Me If I'm a Frog

by Ann Milton

Illustrated by Jill Chambers

Stemmer
House

Publishers
PO Box 89
4 White Brook Rd.
Gilsum, NH 03448
WWW.STEMMER.COM

Inquiries should be directed to:
Stemmer house Publishers
PO Box 89
4 White Brook Road
Gilsum, NH 03448

A Barbara Holdridge book

Printed and bound in Canada
First Edition
Second Printing

Designed by Barbara Holdridge
Composed in Benguiat by Hellen Hom
Printed on acid-free 100 lb. matte paper and bound by Transcontinental Metrolitho

This book is dedicated with love to my mother, Mary Catherine Loretta Schopp Marquette. Her faith and sense of humor have always kept me going. A.M.

Thanks to my brother, Andrew, for all your help in the research. J.C.

Library of Congress Cataloging–in–Publication Data

Milton, Ann, 1942-
    Ask me if I'm a frog / by Ann Milton ; illustrated by Jill
Chambers. -- 1st ed.
        p.   cm.
    "A Barbara Holdridge book"--T.p. verso.
    Summary: Uses questions and explanatory text to compare the
anatomy and habits of a frog with those of a child and discusses the
habitats and life cycles of frogs.
    ISBN 0-88045-140-8 (hardbound). -- ISBN 0-88045-143-2 (pbk.)
    1. Frogs--Juvenile literature. [1. Frogs.]   I. Chambers, Jill,
1961-   ill.   II. Title.
QL668.E2M55   1998
597.8'9--dc21
                                                98-19485
                                                CIP
                                                AC

Are you a frog?

Stick out your tongue. If you have a tongue like a frog, it is long and sticky.

Touch your tongue. Is it sticky?

Can you zap a fly out of the air with your long sticky tongue and swallow it whole?

Are you a frog?

Feel the top of your head.

Are there two bulgy eyes like marbles up there?

A frog's eyes sit on top of its skull – one on each side – so a frog can look in two directions at the same time. It can see a mosquito lunch off to the right and a butterfly dinner coming in from the left without turning its head.

Are your eyes on the top of your head?

Can you see in two directions at once?

Are you a frog?

A frog can't chew. It has only one tiny row of teeth far back in its mouth. To eat a worm or a spider, a frog squishes its eyes closed and pushes and pushes. The pushing makes the frog's eyes go down through the roof of its mouth, and the eyes help shove the food down the frog's throat.

Do you shove your food down your throat with your eyes? Do you eat like a frog? Does your mother like it?

A frog has three eyelids, one on top and two on bottom. One eyelid is clear, like plastic wrap, and the frog can see through it when it is closed. The clear eyelid helps the frog see underwater, and keeps things out of the frog's eyes.

How many eyelids do you have?

Can you see with your eyelids closed?

Are you a frog?

When a frog floats in the
water, just the top of its
head sticks out, but it can see
and breathe, because its eyes and
nose are up there. If just the very
top of your head stuck out of the
water, could you see and breathe?

Feel your ears.

If your ears are like soft shells glued to your
head, and you can stick your fingers in
them, they are not frog ears.

Frogs never have to wash behind their ears
because their ears are skin drums stuck into
the sides of their heads.

Frog's ears hear very, very well. They can hear leaves falling to the ground, and when they're underwater, they can even hear fish swimming.

What kind of ears do you have?

Must you wash behind them?

Do you wish you had frog ears?

Frogs eat their skin. They yawn a big yawn and then they stretch. Their skin splits down the back, and they grab it like a sweater and pull it over their heads. When they get the skin to their mouths, they stuff it in and start swallowing. Down it goes. All done in seconds, and the new skin that was underneath the old skin feels fresher than a shower.

Baby frogs swallow their skin a lot because frog skin doesn't grow, and shedding their skin is the only way they can get bigger. They outgrow skin the way babies outgrow clothes.

Grown up frogs shed their skin because they breathe and drink through it, and skin gets very dirty living around muddy ponds.

How about you? Do you pull your skin over your head and eat it?

Does your skin grow when you do?

Are you a frog?

Is your back green or gray? Is it spotted? Some frogs' backs are. That way critters that like to eat frogs are not able to see them well. Frogs don't like to be seen by rats, or foxes, or hedgehogs. They don't get too close to snakes, gulls, turtles, owls, hawks or weasels, either.

On a cloudy day, frog skin gets darker. On sunny days, it gets lighter. Long ago people told stories about frogs that put on cloaks that made them invisible. They didn't know that frogs were changing color to blend in with things around them.

Can you make your skin change
color so that no one can see
you sitting in the grass or lying in
a shadow?

Check out your belly. Frogs
have pale bellies, so it's
hard for a hungry fish in the
water underneath to look up
and see them.

Is your belly pale?

Sit like a frog.

When a frog's long feet are flat on the floor, the hind legs will fold down so that the knees almost touch the toes. Are you sitting like a frog? Do your knees touch your toes?

Spring into the air.

Long legs, long feet, and ankle joints that bend as easily as a new stick of gum, are great equipment for quick takeoffs. Frogs find it easy to leap straight up in the air from a sitting position.

Can you?

21

Look at your fingers. If you are a frog, you have four fingers. Count them. Do you have the right number of fingers to be a frog?

If you are a frog, you have five toes. Take off your shoes and look at your toes. Frog toes are connected to each other by pieces of skin. Do you have webbing between your toes? Webbed toes help a frog swim fast.

Can you swim fast?

Frogs walk funny because they have short arms. Their arms are only half as long as their legs.

Do you have long legs and short arms? Is it easy for you to walk on your hands and feet at the same time?

adpoles look like bullets with tails until they begin to grow legs, and arms pop out. If a tadpole loses an arm or a leg, no problem – it grows another one. If a full-grown frog loses an arm or leg, though, it is out of luck. One set of arms and legs is all that a grown-up frog gets.

Were you once a tadpole?

Did you come with arms and legs
or did they grow after you
were born?

If you lose an arm
or a leg, can you
grow a new one?

Do you eat stink beetles? You don't? Then you MIGHT be a frog. Frogs think stink beetles taste yucky and frogs would know. Frogs have lots of taste buds—in the roofs of their mouths, in their tongues and in their jaws.

If a frog happens to get something in its mouth that doesn't taste good, it spits it out.

W hen you get something
in your mouth that you don't like,
what do you do?

Do you eat slugs or worms or maggots
or snails or spiders or butterflies?

No?

Then perhaps you are not a frog after all.
These are a frog's favorite foods. They
shove them in their mouths with both
hands and swallow them whole.

Frogs like to sing. Each family of frogs has its own special voice. You may think every frog sings "RIBBET RIBBET" all day, but different kinds of frogs make different sounds.

Green treefrogs sound like the clink of a cowbell. The carpenter frog sounds like a hammer striking nails. The pig frog sounds like a pig grunting.

Cricket frogs sound like crickets. The Florida gopher frog sounds like a man snoring. The barking frog sounds like a dog.

And the croak of some horned frogs sounds like the moo of a cow.

Let me hear you sing.

Do you sound like a frog?

Some frogs like to make loud sounds. They grow elastic skin sacs below their mouths. These sacs swell out like bubble gum bubbles when they sing and make their voices louder.

When a frog is in danger,
it screams
with its mouth
open. Then it
plays dead. Its body
gets stiff and it doesn't
breathe. Many of its enemies
think it is really dead and drop it, but
when the coast is clear, the frog jumps
up and hops away as fast as it can go.

Do you play dead when you are in trouble?

Does it work for you?

Frogs that live in hot places find a cool spot and go into a deep sleep when they get too warm. Frogs that live in cold places find a warm spot and go into a deep sleep when they get too cold. And they don't need an alarm clock to wake up.

When the weather gets just right, the frog's blood goes faster and faster, until the frog feels like hopping up and down and looking around for its friends.

What do you do when the weather feels too hot or too cold for you?

Do you go to sleep?

Do you need an alarm clock to wake up?

Are you a frog?

Well, what do you think?

Do you have bulgy eyes and flat ears?

Is your nose on top of your head?

Do you have a long sticky tongue that catches bugs?

Do you have cute little webbed toes?

Are you a frog?